HUMAN RESOURCE MANAGEMENT

An International and Comparative Perspective

INSTRUCTOR'S MANUAL

Graham Hollinshead & Mike Leat

PITMAN PUBLISHING

PITMAN PUBLISHING
128 Long Acre, London WC2E 9AN

A Division of Pearson Professional Limited

First published in Great Britain in 1995

© G Hollinshead and M Leat 1995

ISBN 0 273 60448 1

British Library Cataloguing in Publication Data
A CIP catalogue record for this book can be obtained from the British Library

10 9 8 7 6 5 4 3 2 1

Printed and bound in Great Britain

The Publishers' policy is to use paper manufactured from sustainable forests.

CONTENTS

Introduction

The major aims of the text, referred to in the preface, are:

To provide an integrated and holistic view of Human Resource Management (HRM) approaches and practices across a range of national systems. The countries we have selected are Germany, France, Italy, the Netherlands, Sweden, the United Kingdom and the United States of America. The rationale underlying the selection of countries is to provide a range wide enough to permit effective cross comparison, yet narrow enough to retain coherence and detail. By selecting this sample of countries, we aim to explore various typologies underlying the employment relationship. It is argued that the typologies manifest broader and diverse ideological and cultural facets of the societies in question.

To embark upon a critical evaluation of HRM after defining the HRM concept, we consider whether it has validity in national systems other than those in which it is widely used, notably the U.S. and the U.K. In doing so, we argue that, particularly in Europe, the roles of government and trade unions have to be brought into the reckoning, as do the processes of interaction between the major interest groups in industry, known as the "Social Partners".

We suggest too that the **value** of taken for granted domestic activity can be scrutinised more closely through taking an international view. In other words, making cross comparisons, and obtaining a fuller picture of HRM and associated practice, can enable us to weigh up more authoritatively the validity of prescriptions for success and for change.

Regarding the structure of the text, in Section 1 we take a thematic approach, addressing in particular, (1) the position of the major "Stakeholders", (2) the processes of interaction between them through participative mechanisms and the formulation of H.R. policy, and (3) the global and national contexts in which they operate. Throughout this section we support analysis with continuous reference to the selected countries. In Section 2 we provide a fuller exposition of HRM frameworks and policies in each of the selected countries. The template we have used for establishing coherence, and for structuring the sequence of material, is the "Harvard model" of HRM formulated by Michael Beer et al in 1984.

In this manual for, Section 1, we shall provide a brief summary of the contents of each chapter, and suggested responses to Discussion questions at the end of each chapter. As Tutors will know, there are few definitive and correct answers in these areas, so, this being the case, we shall highlight key points for discussion where appropriate.

The main text has been designed so that it is "reader-friendly" through the provision of chapter outlines, learning objectives and chapter summaries. We will therefore not duplicate these or other pedagogic mechanisms within the text.

SECTION 1

HRM THEMES AND ISSUES

Chapter 1

Introductory themes and perspectives on the employment relationship

The Chapter may be viewed as comprising of two interrelated sections. The first component considers reasons for engaging in international and comparative analysis from the points of view of "Practitioners" and "Academics". This covers issues such as the globalisation of production, the dominant and influential position of multinational corporations and the Single European Market. Perhaps the key element of rationale here, and one in keeping with the overall orientation of the book, is the notion that to really understand international manifestations of HRM, it is necessary to "dig below the surface" to expose the more profound ideological and possibly cultural explanations for the distribution of power in societies. It is argued, in particular, that the degree to which the exercising of managerial prerogative is tolerated by a society, will affect the characteristics of HRM within that milieu. Emerging from this analysis is the implication that prescriptions for success in HRM may be influenced by powerful, yet scarcely questioned, or perhaps even recognised, ideological and cultural preconceptions.

The second component exposes more fully the major ideological and cultural "theories" underlying HRM essentially, the ideological perspectives, which comprise Liberal Individualism, Liberal Collectivism, Corporatism and Radical are used to explain why in some countries there may be a preference for deregulated, free market orientated policies, which will influence HRM policy choices, whilst in others the tendency will be towards greater state intervention, a sharing of power, and a preference towards Social Partnership. Of course this is an oversimplification, and in discussing ideology the nuances associated with each typology, including the radical perspective, will need more profound consideration.

In discussing culture we draw particularly on the work of Geert Hofstede and specify the cultural dimensions of Power Distance, Uncertainty Avoidance, Individualism, and Masculinity. We note certain reservations about cultural stereotyping, but do observe certain correlations with ideological perspectives. For example, it is noted that in certain "individualistic" societies there may be a preference towards individual payment by results which could be expected to proliferate in the less regulated economies.

Discussion Questions

1   Why should domestic personnel practitioners be interested in learning from abroad?

The section entitled "The Practitioner's viewpoint" contains a number of relevant points in response to this, in summary;

      a)   Globalisation
                Business operations, and HRM decisions do not take place in isolation, and changes in the "world economic order" mean that antennae need to be raised.

In particular changes in Eastern Europe, challenges within the European Union and the growth of Latin American and Pacific Rim economies need to be observed. (Holden 1994)

Due to improvements in technology and communications, amongst other factors, not only is the nature of competition becoming more international, but also the scope for international collaboration and rationalisation of productive facilities to gain economies of scale and thus competitive advantage. (see FT article - GM to sell European luxury car in US).

b)   Multinational Enterprises (MNEs)

These exert a potent influence for a number of reasons;

MNEs can influence domestic practice, for example through "Japanisation"

For those working within MNEs, there are a number of important HR policy issues to be resolved in the areas of reward patterns, succession planning, expatriation, and provision of language training. As well being called upon to give advice in these areas, HR Practitioners should become more internationally mobile themselves.

c)   The Single European Market

Three major challenges are identified which may confront practitioners;

Economic integration has prompted a wave of mergers and amalgamations across a number of sectors. Practitioners may need to manage the implications of organisational restructuring and staff severance.

Freedom of movement of labour has implications for HR planning and recruitment.

The legal measures emanating from Brussels, which impact upon employment, need to be taken on board. (For a more detailed analysis see the chart on pages 314-316.)

In discussing this question it is necessary to bear in mind that "domestic" may be taken to relate to any single country.

2   *What constraints exist on "importing" new HRM ideas from overseas? How may they be overcome?*

A number of the relevant issues for consideration are contained on page 4 in the checklist of points provided by Peter Nicholls on learning from Japan.

In addition, in terms of the practice of transferability, the following types of constraint may be identified.

Suspicion or resistance on the part of the indigenous population to the imposition of "alien" practices.

Restrictiveness on the part of Government towards foreign investment and influence.

Variations in economic, technological, social etc conditions between countries.

Inevitably, the practices of multinational concerns are likely to be raised in pursuing this debate, these are addressed more fully from pages 78 to 84.

It may be instructive to relate these constraints back to the ideological and cultural stereotypes presented in the chapter. It may be argued, for example, that prescriptions associated with Liberal Individualism will not be meaningful or applicable in a Corporatist milieu.

On the question of how to overcome constraints, this may be tackled at a number of levels. At a practical level, debate is likely to focus on how the attitudes and actions of "stakeholders" may be modified. At a more conceptual level, discussion may highlight the following:

methodological improvements in obtaining and interpreting data from overseas.

The extent to which a process of "convergence" is breaking down the ideological and cultural distinctions between national systems. More specifically, the argument may be addressed that the increasingly competitive global market is promoting common and international responses towards deregulation and flexible working practices. The Conclusion (Chapter 20) explores this in more detail.

3 & 4 *From your current knowledge of political/employment systems in different countries, identify at least two countries which fit most closely the four major ideological perspectives identified in this chapter.*

Select four countries with which you are familiar. Would you accept Hofstede's stereotyping in respect of these? Why/why not?

In response to these questions the following matrix is offered to guide discussion. It shows major features of selected countries, and corresponding ideological and cultural tendencies (using Hofstede's indices) of course, the classifications postulated are subject to debate.

Key:

Culture	PDI	Power distance	LI	Liberal individualism
	UAI	Uncertainty avoidance	LL	Liberal collectivism
	IDV	Individualism	C	Corporatism

DIVERSITY IN THE WEST COUNTRIES:
IDEOLOGIES AND CULTURES

	KEY FEATURES	CULTURAL INDICES	IDEOLOGICAL TENDENCY

UK	Emphasis on collective bargaining
	Voluntarist traditions
	Large public sector
	Change:
	    Increased importance of the
	    market
	    Privatisation
	    Decentralisation of collective
	    bargaining
	    Individualism
	    Decline of trade unions
		PDI 35
		UAI 35
		IDV 89
		MAS 66
			LI
			
			LC

US	Legally backed framework Hostility towards trade unions Some collective bargaining Growth of Human Resource Management Deregulation	PDI 40 UAI 46 IDV 91 MAS 62	LI LC
JAPAN	State represents enlarged family Lifetime employment Seniority based wages Enterprise based unions Consensus decisions	PDI 54 UAI 92 IDV 46 MAS 95	 C
NL	Developed welfare state Tripartite decision making Centralised collective bargaining "Pillarisation" on religious/ideological lines Some deregulation	PDI 38 UAI 53 IDV 80 MAS 14	C LC
FRANCE	Large public sector Quite highly regulated Antagonistic industrial relations Bureaucratic Trend towards deregulation	PDI 68 UAI 86 IDV 71 MAS 43	C LC
ITALY	North/south divide Political and religious ideology significant Tripartite decision making Highly regulated employment Centralised collective bargaining Inflation linked wages	PDI 50 UAI 75 IDV 76 MAS 70	C LC

5   *Predict how cultural characteristics of selected countries are likely to influence:*
     (a) organisation design
     (b) approaches to recruitment, remuneration and training and development.

The following provide indications of how cultural dimensions may be tentatively used to predict dominant organisational form or major features of H.R. practice.

Individualism; for countries which are high on individualism we may expect individual performance appraisal, individual payment by results, and individualised career paths. Possibly, selection processes will place an emphasis on individualistic behavioural characteristics.

Power distance; where PDI is high we may expect "taller" organisational structures with fewer consultative mechanisms. Conversely, low power distance may be consistent with "flatter" and more democratic organisational forms.

Uncertainty Avoidance; where UAI is high there will be a preference to avoid risk taking. This may be manifested in more bureaucratic organisational forms, and HR policies in the areas of recruitment, employee development etc geared towards nurturing and retaining staff.

Masculinity; where MAS is high there may be an emphasis on the achievement of status, and the provision of symbols to reflect this, as opposed to policies which will promote welfare and security.

This exercise may be extended to cover the whole gamut of employment policies (possibly in groups) and findings compared with actual practices described in Chapter 2.

Chapter 2

The HRM Concept: An international view

In this Chapter we commence by defining the "Harvard" model of Human Resource Management, which we argue has been influential in subsequent conceptions of HRM. In tracing the origins of the HRM concept we find it significant that its initial prominence occurred in the deregulated economies of the United States and the United Kingdom in the early/mid 1980s. This leads us to observe an association between liberal individualistic ideology and HRM, which we suggest represents a challenge for the organised labour and its representatives. In considering the broader applicability of the HRM concept across a range of national systems, but particularly in Continental Europe, we find that the assumptions underlying liberal individualism may not be sustained, and that in a number of national systems constraints exist on management in formulating HRM policies and practices. Statutory intervention into pay determination and other processes, and a desire or requirement on management to consult union representatives, imply a need to broaden orthodox conceptions of HRM in a European context to take further account of the role of stakeholders in the employment relationship and "situational" factors. In accepting the utility of the Harvard model as the most suitable available template for guiding international analysis, and in using it to provide the framework for the structuring of subsequent material in the text, we nevertheless would suggest modifications to this conception to take into account, in particular, the significance of the "Social Partnership" approach in Europe.

Discussion Questions

1   *Would you accept that the desired HRM consequences of "commitment" and "cost effectiveness" are reconcilable? Is there any conflict between them?*

Debate here may centre around two conflicting propositions;

Firstly, certain widely accepted formulations of HRM (eg Guest (1988)) suggest that policies which encourage employees to identify closely with corporate objectives, and possibly to work "beyond contract" will contribute to enhanced productivity and consequently cost effectiveness.

Secondly, and by way of contradiction, critics of HRM (for example Legge (1989)) argue that matching HRM with business strategy may require labour costs to be minimised, a policy which is hardly consistent with engendering staff commitment. This argument is taken further on pages 21 and 22. HRM and the role of stake holders: contradictions within the concept.

These perspectives may be argued with reference to actual corporate practice.

2   *Would it be beneficial for "stakeholders" in all countries to move towards HRM ? Why/Why not?*

This is an open ended question permitting debate on the following issues;

Is HRM likely to promote tangible rewards for all those involved in it, or may management's gains be at the expense of employees? This debate is taken further from pages 21 to 24 in the sections on HRM and the role of stakeholders and HRM and trade unions.

More generally, is HRM likely to promote improved economic performance? This issue is addressed in Chapter 20 (The Conclusion).

Thirdly, the question may be discussed with reference to the ideological perspectives cited in Chapter 1 and it may be argued that in corporatist or liberal collectivist milieu moves towards HRM would be inappropriate.

3   *Is there a place for trade unions within HRM? If so, what type of role would they play?*

Various conceptions of HRM take different views of the trade union role, ranging from non existent in hard approaches, to being useful facilitators in the management and implementation of change in softer versions. The Harvard model does envisage a role for unions as important stakeholders, but as we suggest in the text the interventions of trade unions may not be welcome if they impede or transgress the transmission of fundamental management beliefs and values, or indeed if they represent a real countervailing power on management. These issues are discussed more fully in the section HRM and trade unions from pages 22 to 24.

Regarding the role of trade unions, HRM initiatives may place unions in a quite invidious position, or appear to marginalise them. Areas such as reward, working arrangements and communication procedures, which have been the subject of joint determination in the past, may, through HRM initiatives, be catered for unilaterally by management. At face value management may seem to be satisfying employee demands in these areas by providing acceptable terms and conditions of employment, and apparently managing the employment relationship in a sophisticated way to the benefit of employees. Claims however that new approaches render trade unions redundant would seem to neglect a fundamental purpose of unions, which is to promote democracy in the workplace and to provide employees with an independent power base. It could well be the case that modern forms of HRM will need to recognise the significant, and potentially useful, role of unions from a management point of view.

4   *What areas of actual practice with regard to recruitment, reward, and training would you associate with HRM? Where possible, quote actual corporate practice.*

John Storey, in Developments in the Management of Human Resources, Oxford, Blackwell, 1992, in carrying out a survey of HR Practice in the UK, provides a useful checklist of indicators of HRM style approaches; In total twenty-five points are included under four headings; beliefs and assumptions, strategic aspects, line management and key levers. For our purposes we shall concentrate on key levers, which relate to areas of HR practice. Our discussion is by necessity selective, and readers are advised to refer to Storey's original

As far as selection is concerned, it would be expected that the significance of this task would increase, it shifting from being a quite marginal activity towards being an integrated key task. Possibly too the use of Psychometric testing could be expected (to test personal attributes such as potential commitment) although in a subsequent survey (The Leicester Training and Enterprise Council survey, reported in HRM A Critical Text 1995, Routledge London and New York) Storey finds that the initially quite modest uptake of Psychometric testing had been discontinued in a number of cases.

For Pay and Conditions the prevalent policy would be towards relationship with performance, and away from multiple fixed grades towards few if any grades. Harmonized conditions may also be expected.

In respect of Training and Development, in the HRM paradigm, "Learning" companies would replace those which controlled access to courses. It is worth noting too that the "Harvard" model places considerable emphasis on Training and Development, linking type of training provision to individual career paths.

These points may be developed in answering this question by citing familiar corporate practices. Storey's (1992) analysis continues to provide an in depth review of change in a cross section of fifteen organisations, and this may be used to supplement discussion.

5 *What are the features of organisations which exemplify the HRM approach in terms of ownership, history, composition of the labour force, nature of business, and industrial relations traditions?*

This discussion could extrapolate from the section entitled HRM as a perspective on the employment relationship (pages 20 and 21) in which we refer particularly to the work of Beaumont, Singh and Hendry and Pettigrew. The following may be postulated as organisational features associated with HRM:

Predominantly (although not exclusively) service sector
Technologically advanced
Marginalised (or non existent trade unions)
White collar (and possibly female)labour
American or Japanese owned or influenced
Relatively large scale

In a more recent piece of work (John Storey, HRM A Critical text) it is suggested that some of these stereotypical factors may be questioned. In particular, it is argued that HRM is quite pronounced in "Traditional" manufacturing and unionised concerns. (P.20)

Chapter 3

The Global and National Contexts

In this Chapter we suggest that there is an element of contingency between external "situational" factors and the formulation of HR policies at an organisational level. The section is effectively divided into two sections; the first part considers global factors under the headings of economic, political, technological demographic and ecological change, whilst the second lays out the specific contexts for each of our selected national systems. We conclude that at an international level, economic and technological changes, and an intensification of competition, are promoting the need for adaptable and flexible organisational responses, whilst distinct national institutional and cultural patterns continue to exist.

Discussion Questions

1   *What forms of organisational flexibility exist? Why are organisations having to become more flexible?*

A useful schema for discussing flexibility may be to divide it into the interrelated classification of functional, numerical and financial flexibility.

Functional flexibility relates to modifications in the divisions between jobs to allow a greater variety of tasks to be carried out.

Numerical flexibility is concerned with variations in the number of staff who are permanently attached to enterprises, and encompasses discussion of part time work etc.

Financial flexibility refers to a relationship between patterns of reward and measures of employee or organisational performance.

For a more detailed analysis of forms of flexibility it would be instructive to consider the work of John Atkinson, for example "Manpower strategies for flexible organisations "Personnel Management 16(8) 1984.

In response to the second part we argue that a range of conjunctural factors are causing organisations to question existing approaches and to see the need to respond effectively to global and national pressures for change. We would note in particular the much heralded product market changes from stable mass to volatile niche, and corresponding changes in production systems sometimes explained by Fordist and Post Fordist paradigms.

2   *What effects do multinationals have on domestic systems of HRM? How do they affect the power of employees?*

In tackling this question it would be worth pointing out that multinational concerns (MNEs) do not exert an homogenous and inevitable influence on domestic systems.

As we point out, much depends upon the strategy of each concern. In this respect, Perlmutter's Ethnocentric, Polycentric and Geocentric typologies may be useful, in examining the extent to which MNEs wish to influence or manipulate HR characteristics within the host country.

Nevertheless it is clear that MNEs can represent an important conduit for the international dispersion of HR practices. American and Japanese concerns in particular have been important in the promotion of ideas such as Just in Time production systems, quality circles, single status conditions of employment and single union deals.

Regarding the impact of MNEs on the power of indigenous employees, a number of points can briefly be made.

Firstly, MNE investment can create jobs in the host country, and may stimulate economic regeneration.

On the more negative side, domestic employees may possess a weak bargaining position due to the ultimate ability of many MNEs to relocate, or transfer investment across national boundaries should labour costs be viewed as excessive, or perhaps if there has been a history of industrial unrest. Related to this, trade unions have only had limited success in establishing international collective bargaining in order to counterbalance MNE power.

A further potential threat to employees is "social dumping". This process involves the location of MNEs in those regions where labour and other costs are lowest, and this may stimulate a downward spiral of wages and other conditions on a domestic and even international basis.

3   *What action should employers take in response to the demographic time bomb?*

The following are possible responses;

Review approaches towards the recruitment and retention of older workers, particularly early retirement.

Tap into relatively untapped pools of labour. This may include women and ethnic minorities.

Review standard working patterns to facilitate the recruitment and retention of the groups identified above.

In a context of growing pressure on the welfare state it may be necessary to consider the provision of private healthcare schemes.

Consider special provisions for those who need to care for the elderly, eg career breaks and flexible working time (for a fuller explanation see section on demographic change from page 34 to 39).

4 *How can cultural and ideological perspectives explain the distinct features of national HRM contexts?*

This question invites readers to establish linkages between actual aspects of the contexts of selected countries outlined in this section and the ideological and cultural typologies outlined in Chapter 1.

By way of general guidance and example we would expect to see the State and its agencies, and the position of trade unions with some priority where Corporatism is a prevalent ideology. Where Liberal Individualist ideas hold sway we may expect to see a more detached state role, and moves such as privatisation of the public sector. In cultural terms, factors such as admiration of individual or collective achievement, preferences for security or risk taking, authoritarian or democratic styles are likely to be significant. A brief pen portrait of most striking cultural characteristics is contained in each of the descriptions of specific national contexts from pages 39 to 70.

Chapter 4

Management, Multinationals, and Employers Organisations

In this Chapter, we consider various features of management, which we note has, in a number of countries, been in an ascendent position over the past couple of decades. It is important to reflect upon management as it may be viewed as the major institutor of HR policy.

The Chapter is divided into three main sections. In the first part we examine typologies of management styles and strategies, which may help us to gain an insight into the philosophy underpinning HRM. We make the point that forms of management style are conditioned by cultural and ideological characteristics of the societies in which they are generated. We then turn to consider the role of Multinational corporations (MNEs). MNEs are major power brokers in international HRM and we go on to consider their impact upon domestic HR systems and organisational culture. Particular attention is given to "Japanisation" as it is argued that Japanese companies have exerted a powerful demonstration effect on domestic companies in the area of HRM.

Finally, we turn to the role of Employers' Associations who, in some countries remain important actors in HRM through, for example, participating in pay determination. Yet, in general, a move towards greater corporate autonomy in aspects of HR policy formulation has been at the expense of Employers Associations.

Discussion Questions

1   What determines different management styles and strategies (a) in different countries and (b) over time?

In responding to this question, it would be useful to define the ideal typologies of management style. These would include unitary and pluralistic as well as the five styles of industrial relations management (Purcell and Gray) contained in table 4.1 on page 76.

At the centre of this question is the notion that forms of management style and strategy are to an extent conditioned by the prevailing ideological and cultural milieu of the societies in which they are generated. Thus, in the chapter, (pages 77 and 78), using the work of Poole (1986), the following examples are given;

Benevolent paternalism in Japan being linked to Confucianism.
Unitary perspectives in the US being linked to a preference for individualism.

This analysis may be supplemented by Gallie's comparative study of oil refineries in France and Britain in 1978. (p.77)

Turning to the issue of evolving management styles over time, in short, an argument may be postulated that highly competitive product markets have brought in their wake

16

more directive and unitary styles of management, and an abandonment of negotiated and pluralistic approaches (see Poole (1981)). Such arguments need to be tempered by the knowledge that corporatist and pluralist styles remain prevalent in many countries.

2   *Is "Japanisation" to be welcomed or resisted?*

On the positive side, the global operation of Japanese concerns has created jobs, and the undoubted efficiency of many of these concerns may have contributed to the wealth of those participating in them. Turning to Japanese organisational practice, clearly practices such as quality circles, harmonised conditions of employment and direct communications offer potential benefits to employees.

At the nub of the question is whether the rather paternalistic styles of "empowerment" associated with Japanese concerns are in fact illusory, in practice offering employees little independent power over fundamental decisions affecting them. It may be the case that working for Japanese concerns suits those who demonstrate the required level of attitudinal commitment towards such enterprises, but not those with a more sceptical disposition.

A checklist of points representing a critique of Japanisation, drawn from Delbridge and Turnbull (1992) is included on page 84.

3   *Do Multinationals necessarily exert homogenising effect on HRM across national systems?*

The answer to this is negative as MNEs are often bound to adapt their approaches to meet the cultural, legal, institutional, political and social conditions and conventions of the countries in which they operate.

4   *What are the requirements for an effective multinational team of managers?*

In responding to this question material can be extrapolated from the newspaper article appearing on page 82 by Jean Louis Barsoux, amongst other sources. We would highlight the following features;

Development of trust(probably over time)
Overcoming stereotypes
Describing differences in a depersonalised way
Use of humour
Capitalising on diversity.

5   *What is meant by "Social Dumping"? How may it be avoided?*

Social Dumping essentially refers to a state of affairs in which an MNE opts to locate in a region where costs, particularly labour costs, are relatively low, this triggering a downward spiral of wages and conditions by other employers who need to match or undercut such rates to remain competitive.

It is likely that Social Dumping would most effectively be tackled through action at a macro international level. Of course, this is likely to involve a clash of ideologies between "free marketeers" and those who would favour some basic regulation of terms and conditions of employment. The Social Chapter of the Maastricht Treaty can be understood as an attempt to avoid a downward spiral of labour cost cutting and deregulation on an international scale.

The issue of Social Dumping is discussed more fully from pages 81 to 83 in the section "The impact of Multinationals on domestic HR systems".

Chapter 5

The Role of Trade Unions

In this Chapter we set out to explain that trades union movements in developed economies have developed differently, they have different objectives and orientations, and structurally they vary on a number of different dimensions. One of the major areas of debate in comparative study has been that concerned with seeking explanation as to why trade union membership figures vary so greatly from one country to another, and in this chapter we address some of the more recent contributions to this debate. This, in turn, emphasises the need to distinguish explanations for trade union density variations on the longitudinal dimension from those which may have comparative value, and indeed from those which may explain the common decline of recent years.

Underlying these explanations is an acknowledgement that unions are often secondary and responsive organisations confronted by environmental change and threat which in many respects they seem ill-equipped for. Nevertheless, we do not conclude that unions are capable only of reaction, they are not merely passive participants in the system. They, like the other main actors, have the capacity to make choices and take initiatives which at the least can mitigate the threatening effect of many of the changes confronting them.

Discussion Questions

1 Examine the main points of difference between "business" and "welfare" trades union movements.

The main points of difference between "business" and "welfare" movements can be examined on a number of dimensions, eg

	Business	Welfare
Political affiliation	No	Yes
Class based	No	Yes
Prime focus		
Subject matter	Terms and conditions	Social transformation/policy
Level	Local	National
Method	Collective Bargaining +	Political activity +
Structure	Decentralised	Centralised

It is important that students appreciate that the above represents ideal types and that, in reality, the differences may be neither so extreme or clear.

2 To what extent is the traditional business-welfare distinction adequate as a typology in the world of the 1990s?

Arguably the traditional typology is no longer adequate, as is indicated in the chapter by reference to the possible emergence of a third group characterised perhaps by its stature as a social partner.

There is evidence that the traditional "business" movements of Japan and the USA are becoming more politicised and more aware that to be effective on behalf of their members, they need to be active and organised above and beyond the level of the immediate workplace so that they may, for example, counter the implications of: increased internationalism in economic activity and the scope of company activities and product markets, national level economic management priorities and options, and to exert pressure for an appropriate and sympathetic regulatory framework.

There is also evidence that those "welfare" movements that in a sense have remained "purest" in form as for example in France and Italy, are being forced to confront the developing interests and concerns of employees in the workplace and in new constituencies. In some circumstances they have been encouraged to develop new mechanisms and structures for representing these interests locally. Sometimes this is a response to membership activity and pressure but as often these developments are in response to employers' determination to implement locally greater flexibility and discretion in terms and conditions of employment and working practices, sometimes aided and abetted by governments increasingly concerned with issues of international competitiveness to which such flexibility, coupled with deregulation, may seem an attractive alternative.

The business-welfare typology is perhaps now best viewed as representing the opposite ends of a spectrum between which there is scope for a range of "types" combining in varying degrees elements of the characteristics of the extremes.

3   *How might developments in the external technological and economic/market contexts influence trade union (a) objectives and (b) structure?*

(a) It is suggested that trade union objectives are influenced by the state of technology when they emerged, with the nature of production systems and associated work organisation influencing the perceived need/desire to transform society. In modern times, it is argued that the rapid rate and colossal implications of technological change, with its impact upon work organisation, employee security and terms and conditions of employment encourages an orientation towards the workplace and bread and butter issues. Examples might be technological change facilitating team production techniques, just-in-time stocking/production, job enrichment and enlargement programmes etc., all of which it is argued encourage employees and their unions to concentrate upon local and immediate issues and objectives.

To the extent that developments in the economic context emphasise/necessitate competitiveness, speed of response, flexibility of product and skill, and internationalism, then again it is likely that employees and unions will be forced to orient their activities towards the workplace and bread and butter issues concerning themselves with job protection and employee security.

An alternative view might be that internationalism, competition and technological

20

change all greatly increase the need for action at the centre in the form of protective government regulation and the creation of frameworks within which objectives can then be pursued locally, so that the same external developments can often generate pressure leading in a number of different directions.

(b) One obvious way in which technological and market developments can impact upon trade union movement structures is when it/they result in demand for new trades, skills or industries or alternatively the demise of established ones. Movements traditionally structured around crafts and extractive and heavy manufacturing industries have experienced massive structural change via mergers and amalgamation with some unions simply ceasing to exist. In many countries union movements can be seen to be moving towards a structure which contains fewer, larger, general or hybrid unions with their own internal regional and trade or industry structures. These developments may also encourage a concern with administrative efficiency and obtaining economies of scale through centralisation. Increased scale may also facilitate effective activity (requiring organisation) on a national level.

However, as noted earlier in the commentary on this question, technological and market change may also be emphasising objectives and activity in the workplace and the effective pursuit of these objectives, the effective protection of employee interests and response to management initiatives, necessitates effective local organisation.

The implications of this commentary might well be that these external developments are impacting upon union movements in a manner which suggest that they need both effective central and local organisation centred upon particular occupational or industrial groupings.

It is debatable whether these developments alone will impact upon political or religious fragmentation.

4 *Examine factors that might encourage trades unions to develop (a) centralised structures (b) decentralised structures?*

The degree of centrality is of course only one dimension of structure, others being membership base and the degree of fragmentation and coherence.

It is also important to always bear in mind that unions are secondary and to some extent reactive organisations when it comes to structural determination. They inevitably seek to organise within an industrial structural context that is already determined.

Nevertheless, they do have choice as evidenced, for example, by the dispute in the USA in the 1930's between those who wanted to organise on an industrial base and those who wanted to pursue an essentially craft base.

Structures can also be complex with various mixes of the above dimensions possible. When discussing centralised/decentralised, it is important to emphasise that no movements are completely one or the other. Inevitably, again, we are discussing emphasis and degree. All national movements operate and organise at more than one level. When we say a movement is centralised or decentralised, we are almost always referring to the dominant level or focus, and not implying exclusivity. This dominance can also vary over time.

What then are the factors/influence that can be seen to encourage either centralisation or decentralisation? Examples might be:

Centralisation	Decentralisation
Political or welfare type objectives	Business/bread and butter objectives
Consensual or corporatist ideology dominant	Liberal collectivist/liberal individualist/neo-laisser faire ideology dominant
Employers wishing to prevent wage competition in an industry and willing to combine and determine industry (or region) wide terms and conditions	Employers who feel able to cope on their own, or who are fiercely independent and competitive and wish to pursue initiatives and strategies at the level of the firm/workplace. Delayering, closeness to the customers, creating local profit/cost centres
Unions in which administrative efficiency outweighs concerns for democracy	Unions in which the concern for democracy encourages decentralised decision-making
Stable technology and mass production systems	Technological change, batch, flexible and specialised production systems

5 *How would you explain the decline in trade union membership experienced in many countries in the last 10-15 years?*

In discussing this question, it is important to seek, to distinguish those influences which appear to have a general and cross-national impact from those which may be country specific.

In the former category, it seems that there is a measure of agreement that one could include:

(i)   structural changes in industry and the labour force occasioned by structural changes in demand, international competition and technological innovation;

(ii) increased unemployment often in industries and skill and occupational sectors traditionally amenable to trade union organisation and inter-related with (i) above;

(iii) enhanced use of "atypical" employment contracts implying and facilitating greater flexibility in the use of labour, e.g. part-time and temporary contracts, replacing permanent and full-time employment and posing logistical and organisational problems for unions.

Within individual countries, one may find a range of other influences having a particular impact, to include:

(i)   the ideology, economic and social priorities of government;

(ii) an enhanced determination on the part of employers to resist trades unionism and pursue anti-union policies;

(iii) the activities and attitudes of the unions themselves and the vigour and effectiveness with which they organise and provide employees with the opportunity to join, and

(iv) the encouragement and development of values and attitudes congruent with individualism and enterprise but not collectivism.

The particular mix of these influences and the scale of their impact demonstrably varies from one country to another.

6 *Consider the prospects for cross or international trades union associations and structures.*

In recent years, the prospects for international trade union confederations (the 2 main ones being the ICFTU and ETUC) and structures have arguably been improved by:

the demise of communism as a force in Europe;
the strengthening of the role of the social partners within the European Union and the specific legislative intervention encouraging European level works councils in Community scale undertakings;
the continuing expansion of the cross-national activities of international companies;
the continuing activities of and forum provided by the ILO encouraging cross-national contact, discussion and co-operation.

However, there are still many obstacles to overcome. National movements are not always coherent, there is plenty of scope still for ideological differences to influence the capacity for agreement on objectives and strategies. Employers, apart from a few internationals, have shown no great willingness to consult, let alone bargain with federations of unions representing their employees across national boundaries. Movements towards decentralisation of decision making create further difficulties. The potential scope of cross-national collective bargaining is also limited by national variations of traditions, legislation and living standards.

Prospects seem greatest within the European Union, but there is opposition from employers and member state governments and any movement to the right of the political spectrum is likely to hamper these prospects further, particularly as it may be necessary to rely upon regulation if substantial future progress is to be made.

7 *Explain the implications of 'ideology' upon trades union objectives, structure and membership.*

Ideology or beliefs and values whether radical, corporatist, or liberal collectivist inevitably influence a union's objectives, what it seeks to achieve, what seems legitimate and desirable. At the extremes of the spectrum referred to in this chapter this may range from unilateral employee control of the labour process and a socialist society at one end to achieving control over the job and negotiating terms and conditions of employment with management at the other. The former extreme of objective is consistent with a radical ideology whereas the latter is not. The radical may reject collective bargaining as a means of decision making since it ensures the continuation of the capitalist status quo reinforcing managerial prerogative whereas others embrace collective bargaining as the preferred means for achieving consensus through compromise.

Radical movements have tended to emphasise centrality given their desire to reform capitalist societies though the more revolutionary still tend to emphasise organisation and activity of the rank and file. The more moderate movements of a corporatist nature are also likely to emphasise centrality since they seek to play an active role in the central determination and implementation of industrial, social and economic policy. However, many such movements have not lose sight of the need to organise and be active and effective at lower levels. The other extreme in the constrained ideological spectrum being dealt with here, the liberal collectivist, is much more likely to focus upon local organisation and activity often, although not necessarily, almost to the exclusion of central structures and mechanisms at the level of the industry or national system.

Ideology influences membership perhaps most apparently at the ideological extremes. At the radical end where compatibility of belief is perhaps more important and likely to constitute a major motive for membership, and where also the centralist orientation may result in a virtual absence of local level organisation and activity, potentially making membership more "difficult" to achieve and sustain. At the other end where individualism dominates, "believers" are unlikely to enter into trade union membership given the inherent collectivism.

There are of course a number of ideological positions not encompassed above and it should not be too difficult to examine the implications of any particular one as long as you appreciate that quite often a particular set of values and beliefs throws up apparently inconsistent implications. It is not always as simple as the above might indicate.

8 *How would you explain the relatively minor variations in the international rank order of national trade union membership density figures over time?*

The relative consistency of the cross-national rankings referred to in this question have encouraged most commentators to look for country specific explanations arguing that while there may be international developments which influence levels of membership in all countries, the comparative rankings can only be explained by differing national characteristics. Trade union membership density is the product of trade union presence, availability and organisation and within any country this can be seen to be influenced by the strategic choices made by the various main actors. It seems likely that there are inter-relationships between these choices and their outcomes and various dimensions of national culture as well as with country size, economic and industrial concentration and social homogeneity, the variables identified by Visser are of particular significance. Other explanations of cross-national variations in membership density which may contribute to an understanding of the relative longitudinal constancy in comparative ranking are trade union participation in the administration of social security and benefit schemes, and also the strength and effectiveness of local level organisation, each of which can be seen as outcomes of particular strategic choices taken within a national cultural context.

There are country specific characteristics which provide an environment within which national actors take decisions on policies and strategies which appear to influence national levels of trade union membership density. Within a country, membership may vary from year to year and there may be common international movements such as the decline in membership in recent years, but the constancy of cross-national ranking can only adequately be explained by acknowledging that there are country specific features and influences at work.

Visser J. (1993): "Union organisation: why countries differ", the International Journal of Comparative Labour Law and Industrial Relations, Autumn, pp 206-221.

9 *Examine the suggestion that influences for convergence in the role and structure of trades unions movements in different countries can be significantly mitigated by the strategic choices of the unions themselves.*

Various references have already been made to those influences which may be seen to be "common" across national boundaries and which therefore arguably encourage convergence of role and structure, a similarity of response. Certainly if one adopted a deterministic perspective, one would be likely to view the prospects of such convergence as high, but this perspective implies that trades unions and indeed other actors in industrial relations systems are relatively passive recipients or participants, and it is not a view with which we concur. The alternative view is that national contexts of a cultural, social, economic, political and legal nature serve to both inform and facilitate choice on the part of the actors (choices as to both objective and strategy) and that these "strategic choices" serve to mitigate the potentially deterministic and convergent pressures.

The influences for convergence would include:

(i) Change in structure of demand
(ii) Change in technology and production systems
(iii) Change in structure of industry and labour force
(iv) New employer strategies, i.e. decentralisation, labour flexibility, individualism, involvement and commitment, co-operation
(v) Enhanced international competition.

Arguably these influences encourage trades unions to make structural adjustments which: accommodate the decline of certain skills, occupations and industries and the emergence of new services, industries and occupational groupings; ensure that they have effective organisation and representation at the "new" levels of decision making; seek coherence in place of traditional fragmentation.

In terms of role, these "convergent" influences all tend to point unions in the direction of co-operation rather than conflict, where they pursue a "productionist", "co-operatist" or "constructive" role.

Yet, the unions do have choices. For example, they can refuse to co-operate, they can continue to militantly resist and contest, they can develop alternative strategies and structures, they can structure themselves to counter centrally what they perceive as threats, continuing to seek protection from regulation at a national or international level rather than enter into co-operative arrangements locally. They can pursue with vigour the recruitment and retention of new members in new industries and occupations, or they can decline with the industries, crafts and occupations that were once the source of their strength.

Chapter 6

Government Influences on HRM

Governments can influence human resource systems and management in many different ways and in this chapter we have identified and explained many of them. We acknowledge that government exerts its major influence through its roles as employer and legislator and in its efforts to influence the labour market, even though in many instances the influence is of an indirect nature and the product of actions and decisions taken for motives more commonly concerned with the pursuit of particular economic and social policies.

We identify the significance of perspective and ideology since these underpin and explain many particular government policies and initiatives. Governments, whilst the only actor able to unilaterally change the rules, are by no means completely free agents. They also are constrained by socio-economic, cultural and technological contexts at the same time as they provide part of the context for the other actors. However, government is often in a position to be potentially the most coherent and powerful of the actors and this renders the choices made particularly significant, even when the choice is to do nothing.

We examine some of the influences, arguably encouraging convergence in national systems and practices and note that in our view government, like the other actors, is able to partially mitigate the impact of these convergent influences.

Discussion Questions

1 *Examine why the values, beliefs and perspectives of those elected to govern are important influences upon HRM.*

The values, beliefs and perspectives of government are important because they significantly influence:

(i) the kind of society they consider desirable, for example overtly pluralist and democratic or totalitarian;
(ii) their attitude towards government as an actor, the role they should play and their willingness to intervene;
(iii) their willingness to enter into political exchanges with the other actors in formal or informal bi- or tri-partite arrangements;
(iv) their social, industrial and economic policy objectives, priorities and preferences

and these all provide part of the HRM context.

These values etc. can be seen therefore to indirectly influence the processes and outcomes of employee relations, indirectly because governments rarely intervene or act in order to achieve specific employee relations or HRM objectives. It is more common that in the pursuit of particular economic or industrial objectives, action may be deemed necessary to influence or regulate HR processes or outcomes, or alternatively that there are consequences for the latter from actions in other directions and arenas. Examples are given in this chapter.

As Crouch* has pointed out, governments are the only ones able to unilaterally change the rules of the game.

* Crouch, C (1992) *The Politics of Industrial Relations*, 2nd ed., Fontana, p.146

2 *Distinguish briefly between the liberal and capitalist contexts.*

Discussion of the difference between these 2 contexts should build upon the exposition on pages 7-10 inc. as well as the content of this chapter.

Briefly:

Liberal context: this is one in which individual freedom and choice is emphasised; in which conflicts that occur, for example between buyer and seller, should be resolved through the market mechanism. In its purest form, this context assumes a rough equality of bargaining power between buyers and individual sellers of labour, and therefore regards collective action as an unnecessary and illegitimate regulation of the market. There are similarities between these assumptions and those underlying models of perfect competition. The "collectivist" variant acknowledges the unreality of this assumption of rough equality between buyer and seller and recognises the need for and legitimacy of collective action on the part of the two parties as long as the parties are still able to freely resolve the conflicts between them.

The corporatist context: rejects the assumptions of liberalism as to freedom, choice and the market, and seeks to replace them with integrative mechanisms through which government plays an active role as one of the interested parties in mediating and resolving conflicts amongst them. This context envisages a very much more active and interventionist role for government and the other parties may be either invited to participate voluntarily in integrative mechanisms, or at the other extreme, coerced into participation.

3 *Examine and illustrate the various roles that governments play and ways in which they can influence HRM.*

The roles government plays are variously categorised but certainly encompass those of:

Employer
Legislator
Active labour market intervention, and
Providing other services such as research, advice and conciliation and/or arbitration.

Examples

As **employers** government can influence HRM processes and outcomes in numerous ways, examples of which are:

recognising, or not recognising, trades unions;
agreeing, or not, to collective bargaining and its scope;

determining organisational structures, e.g. encouraging decentralisation of decision making or the separation of purchase from provision of services;
encouraging an emphasis upon management by objectives and performance measurement + appraisal;
encouraging equality of access and treatment;
encouraging management to make more flexible use of labour.

In its **legislative** role, government can:-

protect and further, or discourage, particular interests;
reinforce managements claim to unilateral control;
encourage employee involvement programmes;
outlaw collective bargaining;
mandate particular forums of industrial democracy and employee participation;
regulate terms and conditions of employment such as hours of work;
regulate recruitment and selection procedures;
restrict management's right to terminate employment;

Governments seeking to play an active labour market role have also a number of alternatives open to them. They can:-

Encourage more people to enter the labour market by offering incentives to work, such as reducing unemployment benefits or marginal tax rates.

Make it easier for people to find work via effective job search services and assist with various forms of mobility benefits.

Improve the quality of the labour force through a whole range of education and training initiatives and schemes.

Encourage demand via offering employers subsidies to employ more labour or to do so in a particular locality.

Create jobs via public expenditure schemes, often of a capital nature.

The above are just a selection of the initiatives governments can take in their various roles.

4 *Consider the arguments for and against government allowing and disallowing public sector trades unionism.*

There are a range of arguments for and against, some of which are public sector specific and some of which are of more general relevance. Perspective is obviously relevant.

It is important that a distinction is maintained, as far as possible, between trades unionism and what trades unions might do, e.g. engage in collective bargaining and/or take industrial action. While unions will usually want to participate in decision making via collective bargaining etc. it needs to be borne in mind that membership of a trade union is possible without joint decision making and strikes as inevitable consequences.

28

Examples

Arguments in favour:

(i) Freedom and democracy, essentially that in a free and democratic society, individuals should have the right to form and join a collective and have that collective represent them.

(ii) Governments as employers are no less likely to seek to exploit their employees than are any other.

(iii) Employees of government need representation even more than any other because their employer can unilaterally change the rules.

(iv) Governments change and employees need protection from the sudden changes in policies and practices that may ensue.

Arguments against:

(i) Governments are elected to govern and it is inappropriate to allow trades unions to challenge this;   public sector employers should have unfettered unilateral prerogative, a challenge to this ....

(ii) Trades unions are political organisations and will introduce conflict and dissent into the workplace and seek to pursue political objectives through their members.

(iii) Trades unions constitute an alternative focus for employee loyalty and this is inappropriate in services where "loyalty" to the sovereign or the country is important.

(iv) They are unnecessary because governments cannot afford to treat their employees poorly since they are also voters.

5 *Examine the suggestion that government should seek to act as a model employer, setting an example which private sector employers should follow.*

This is another area or issue upon which perspective and values are likely to be relevant. Those of a liberal persuasion for example might argue that the question is an irrelevance in that government, like all other employers, should be guided by the market.   Equally important is the appreciation that the term model is itself value laden and dependent upon perspective.   I might think a model employer should recognise trades unions and share power because my framework of values is pluralist and democratic, whereas you might think a model employers should resist trades unionism because you have an essentially unitarist value set.

It is the case that governments have performed this role in various countries, sometimes deliberately and sometimes not.   It is less common that the role of model has extended to rates of pay, public sector rates often following comparable private sector rates - a kind of continuous catching-up process.   However, in many countries, governments do try and influence the "going rate" of pay increases by exerting downward pressure on their employees when they are pursuing economic policies geared towards controlling inflation and limiting public expenditure.

It is much more common that governments have consciously tried to set an example of "good" practice in areas of non-wage terms and conditions (e.g. pensions and sickness leave and pay) and employment practices and procedures. In many countries governments as employers have been in the forefront of the fight against discrimination at work and in promoting employment practices that accord with the principles of natural justice.

You might come to the conclusion that governments of whichever "colour" are always likely to utilise the opportunities afforded them as major employers to encourage, by example, private sector employers in the pursuit of what they consider desirable. Whether the behaviour and activities of government in this regard is successful is another question.

6 *Explain and illustrate what is meant by governments intervening in order to create positive rights, and what might the alternatives be?*

Governments as legislators can create via statutory intervention either positive rights, obligations, freedoms and immunities.

As noted in this chapter, the UK was for many years the odd one out of the countries examined in detail in the text, since government had tended not to intervene in a statutory fashion and the law surrounding the employment relationship was a mix of obligations, duties, freedoms, immunities and rights, but derived not from specific statutory intervention but from common law and the law of contract and tort.

In other countries it was much more common for employees and employers to have been granted positive rights and in many instances the most basic of these had been incorporated into a Bill of Rights or Constitution, examples being the right to join a trade union, and the right to take industrial action.

Until very recently in the UK, employees have not had such positive rights. They have had freedoms: the freedom to take industrial action and the freedom to join trades unions. Positive rights can extend to collectives and other legal entities in addition to individuals.

In the last 30 years, governments in the UK have intervened much more commonly to create positive rights by statutory means, sometimes as the result of EU Directives, examples of which could include:

Rights to equal treatment and pay
Rights as members of trades unions
Rights to information upon employment
Rights to redundancy pay.
Rights to consultation viz. collective redundancies
Rights in a health and safety context, and
Rights to maternity leave and pay and a right to return to work.

If you wish to distinguish positive from negative rights, then you could see as negative:

The right not to be unfairly dismissed
The right not to be discriminated against, and

The right not to be unfairly disciplined or expelled from a trade union, and it is a moot point whether the creation of a negative right (the right not to be treated in a particular way) simultaneously creates a positive right, and you could ask your students to debate this. For example:

Does the right not to be unfairly dismissed create a right to be dismissed fairly? And the right not to be discriminated against create a right to be treated equally?

7 *Explain how governments may seek to influence both the supply of and demand for labour.*

It is important at the outset to ensure that students appreciate that there are both quality and quantity and macro and micro dimensions to this question. These dimensions can be used to construct structures or frameworks for dealing with this question. You could also seek to distinguish those policies or initiatives which have a direct impact from those whose impact is indirect. If you wanted to narrow the task for individual students, you could ask them in small groups to classify their answers using just one of these pairs of criteria. Allocate each of the pairs of criteria to a group and once they have each completed this task, they can be brought back together to compare the outcomes of their deliberations and they can be further encouraged to try and devise more complex matrices which seek to combine the pairs of criteria. Examples might be plotting the macro-micro dimension against that concerning the "directness" of impact or perhaps the simple supply-demand dimension or supply-demand against quality and quantity.

There are such a range of initiatives available to governments and for students to identify and explain that, they should have relatively little trouble in gathering together some lists. There are many examples mentioned in the chapter, although it may be advisable to remind them that the demand for labour is one derived from the demand for its product.

8 *Explain by comparing two countries the significance of ideology upon government pursuit of active labour market policies.*

There is plenty of information within the chapter to enable students to answer this question. They should be advised to choose countries which exhibit ideological contrasts, e.g. the USA or UK, compared with say Sweden, Germany or the Netherlands.

The term "active" poses some problems of definition and distinction and to us it seems reasonable that it should imply action, and hence apply to behaviour which is to some extent interventionist, and at the same time there is an implication of directness between the action and its effect. Therefore, active policies are in this case likely to encompass those which are interventionist directly in the labour market and which seek to directly influence one or other element in the market.

To illustrate this, government programmes to directly influence the quality and quantity of labour supply via training and retraining initiatives would qualify, as would expenditure to create jobs and direct subsidy schemes. However, running or allowing a budget deficit at a macro level in order to encourage growth and employment through an expansion of aggregate demand would not so qualify.

Inevitably the edges of these distinctions are blurred and students can benefit from thinking through which initiatives and policies are active and devising their own boundaries through discussion and agreement.

9 In what ways might governments impact upon the likelihood of human resource systems converging across national boundaries?

Essentially the arguments in favour of convergence are derived from global/international developments in markets, technology, production systems etc., the contention being that these will imply:

(i)   common forms of organisation including systems for communication, evaluation and reward;
(ii) common employment practices, human resource initiatives and outcomes, and
(iii) common systems of regulation/deregulation.

Against this convergence there are those who see the actors, institutions, traditions, culture etc. of national systems as mediating influences.

If one accepts the essence of the convergence thesis, then governments will have little mediating impact and may well find themselves performing a different and diminished role.

The converse view sees governments (depending in part upon their ideology) capable of significant mitigation of the convergent influences. The constructive and competitive flexibility models of Grahl and Teague* illustrate this viewpoint particularly aptly. For this mitigation role government have the full range of legislative, regulatory and deregulatory mechanisms available as well as those of economic management. Whether government chooses to mitigate convergent tendencies will depend upon its perception of their desirability and congruence with their own priorities and objectives.

Within the European Union, governments have opportunities to create/encourage or resist convergence of national systems across national boundaries. An extension of qualified majority voting limits the ability of an individual government to influence decisions for or against convergence.

The argument that the market will itself over time lead towards convergence relies upon the removal of barriers to the mobility of resources. In the case of labour, there is relatively little evidence so far that the removal of such barriers is either extensive or imminent.

* Grahl J & Teague P (1991) 'Industrial Relations Trajectories and European Human Resource Management', in Brewster C and Tyson S (eds) *International Comparisons in Human Resource Management*, Pitman, p.67-91.

Chapter 7

Employee Participation

We use the term employee participation broadly to encompass both individual and collective mechanisms through which employees may have the opportunity to influence decisions within organisations. We identify a range of dimensions to participation upon which comparative analysis can be undertaken.

In determining the framework for our comparisons, we emphasise the relevance and importance of the "realness" or "genuineness" of the participation. If the mechanism does not provide a genuine opportunity for employees or their representatives to influence decisions before they are made or veto them afterwards, then arguably it is not a participative mechanism.

We concentrate upon the two most common forms of and forums for employee participation, those being collective bargaining and consultation, but we also do examine other participatory mechanisms - quality circles, team working and some forms of industrial democracy, and we assess the use of these in our base countries. We note the environmental pressures in the direction of decentralisation and identify the prospects for employee participation through collective bargaining and consultation, at a multi-national level.

Discussion Questions

1 Explain the relevance of "purpose" to distinctions between employee participation, involvement and industrial democracy.

Purpose is only one of the dimensions used to try and identify distinctiveness to the various terms in the question. On this criteria or dimension:

(i) Employee participation is viewed as a process which has conflict resolution or joint determination and/or administration as a purpose, or at least a possible outcome. The nature of the process may be conflictual or co-operative, distributive or integrative. It is the jointness of the intended outcome that distinguishes it from the others.

(ii) Employee involvement is a term used to categorise schemes and programmes almost always initiated by management for purposes associated with employee commitment, productivity, performance, efficiency, competitiveness and quality. The purpose is not "jointness" in decision making or in administration.

(iii) Industrial democracy is the term used to depict those arrangements which have as their purpose a genuine sharing of power between all employed stakeholders, often also referred to as systems of worker control or self-management. Arguably some schemes embracing self-managing teams are examples of the term when purpose is the base of the distinction, although they also often have additional purposes more akin to those in (ii) above.

In this area distinctions are rarely clear and simple.

2 Consider whether employee participation necessarily implies that managerial prerogative is limited by the process.

Answers to this question will vary according to interpretation and definition. It is important that students think about how they interpret or define the term employee participation - what does it mean to them?   Which of the many interpretations included in this chapter seem most appropriate or useful.

We adopt a broad, reasonably all-encompassing definition, which embraces employee involvement, collective bargaining and industrial democracy. However, we do also point to the significance of whether participation is real, whether there is in fact an opportunity for employees, individually or collectively, to at least influence a decision before it is made or veto it afterwards. In this sense employee participation must limit management's unilateral decision making, to some extent the decision making becomes bilateral.

However, if you define prerogative as implying a right by virtue of position, then the term managerial prerogative implies that management have or claim a right to decide unilaterally. In this case many of the mechanisms of participation included within a broad definition do not imply a limiting of managerial prerogative. Certainly those schemes that usually fall within the term industrial democracy would be seen to limit it in that employees are granted a "right" to be involved in decision making. Whether collective bargaining limits this prerogative is arguable. Some would say that management voluntarily agree to a limit on their prerogative when they agree to enter into collective bargaining, while others would argue not since management do not necessarily give up their right to not reach agreement and decide unilaterally. Where managements agree to go to arbitration then they are giving up their prerogative.

3 Can Flanders' perception of collective bargaining be integrated into Chamberlain and Kuhn's model of its nature and functions?

Flanders viewed collective bargaining as a process of joint job regulation, the outcome being jointly determined substantive and procedural rules. This is similar to Chamberlain and Kuhn's middle form or stage in the development of collective bargaining which they refer to as "governmental" in nature and define as a process of joint law making implying a sharing of power. Both views are consistent with the view that the outcome of collective bargaining is a jointly determined constitution.

4 Explain why some of the radical perceptions see collective bargaining as a process which employers should avoid.

Employees should not enter into collective bargaining arrangements according to radical perspectives because it is a process which by seemingly sharing decision making power lures employees into a false truce in what should be a continuing war to overthrow capitalism, to replace minority control of the labour process by the bourgeoisie with control by labour itself. The effect of collective bargaining is in fact to perpetuate the status quo of capitalism and managerial prerogative.

Arguably, if one considers that each side in the struggle over the price of labour and control of the labour process ultimately seeks unilateral control, then employers also ought not to enter into any arrangements which limit that unilateralism. To the extent that collective bargaining does impose such limits, employers in their own interest ought not to become involved. They certainly should not agree to any form of arbitration.

A very brief outline of such radical perspectives is given on page 10.

5 *Examine the various influences upon bargaining level and highlight those that might encourage bargaining at a multi-employer level.*

There are many influences upon the level at which bargaining takes place within any national system and explanations of why particular levels dominate. The following is a list of most of the major influences as identified so far:

(i)   the preferences and choices of the parties themselves;
(ii) the size and type of "industry", the number and size of employers and their geographic dispersion, the degree of competition within the product market;
(iii) the number and nature of the trades unions, their membership base;
(iv) the scale of the labour market;
(v)   the approach of government and legislation;
(vi) the time at which collective bargaining developed and the nature of the industry at that time;
(vii)   the size of the country;
(viii)   the need for speed and flexibility in decision making;
(ix) the nature of the technology and rate of change.

As noted in the text, the circumstances or combination of factors that might encourage multi-employer bargaining could include:

(i)   a government keen to achieve consensus and to integrate the various and competing interests;
(ii) an industry or occupation in which there is a strong single trade union representative of the membership and with appropriate means of control and willing to be competitive and engage in pattern bargaining;
(iii) an industry comprised of a reasonably large number of competitive producers or suppliers and where the advantages of combining together outweigh "natural" competitive instincts and the desire individually to be in control;
(iv) a national labour market;
(v)   a small to medium sized country so that multi-employer activity is logistically achievable, and
(vi) relatively stable market and technological environments.

6 *Consider the prospects for collective bargaining at a cross-national level.*

There are 3 cross-national levels at which collective bargaining could take place:

sectoral
multi-sectoral
within one company or group of companies.

Many commentators have identified the various common pressures encouraging management to seek to decentralise collective bargaining, and such pressures can be seen as harming or reducing the prospects for international bargaining activity.

These pressures include the impact of new technology and greater international competition in increasingly globalised markets encouraging employers to seek enhanced flexibility and speed of response, thereby necessitating decision making closer to the point of production and to the customer.

Any decline in the incidence of collective bargaining as a joint rule making process is likely to also discourage international bargaining.

Also acting as negative influences must be differing economic, social and cultural characteristics of national systems, and the absence of effective organisation at a cross-national level. On the assumption that trades unions are the more likely to instigate the development of collective bargaining at this level, it is arguably beholden on them to initiate and develop the essential cross-national relationships and structures. Given the difference of objective, structure and membership density and characteristics, there are significant obstacles to be overcome.

Developments within the EU with particular respect to the new procedures introduced by the Maastricht agreements which give the social partners the opportunity to seek to determine policy by collective bargaining are on the surface more promising. At the least this will (should) give a boost to the development of effective and appropriate organisation. The agreement by all the member states (except the UK) to encourage information and consultation arrangements within community scale (multi-national) companies, and that unions and employers may negotiate arrangements themselves rather than have a particular form imposed upon them, should also prove a positive influence.

Given the significant cross-national differences in living standards and costs, it does seem probable that the best prospects are for the joint determination of principles, procedures and frameworks rather than wage rates and other substantive terms and conditions, either within multi-nationals or particular industrial sectors.

The bottom line, however, is that the parties themselves must want it.

7 *Assess the proposition that joint consultation requires an integrative or co-operative approach from the participants.*

Joint consultation, like collective bargaining, varies considerably in scope, level and nature. The essence of the process is that two or more parties express and exchange information, views and opinions prior to issues being decided. In many systems, joint consultation between employers and employees or their representatives is legally "required" on particular issues.

"Integrative" in this context refers to consensual, co-operative approaches which may have the capacity to produce gains for both parties, often through joint efforts at problem solving and some sharing of the benefits. The converse of integrative is distributive which depicts an approach and relationship which is essentially conflictual, power based and concerned with determining the distribution between the parties of a relatively fixed resource.

As for the proposal in the question, the suggestion is that joint consultation "requires" an integrative approach etc. It may well be that joint consultative activities which are concerned with resolving or devising solutions to particular problems, do "require" such an approach if the full potential benefit is to be derived. In fact, it is arguable that if the process is to be effective, such an approach is always desirable, if not "required", and this applies whether the purpose is specifically problem solving or simple communication in order to satisfy a legal requirement.

Naturally reactions to this proposal may vary with perspective and radical perspectives would view such co-operation with even less relish than the conflict based power play of collective bargaining.

8 *What have been the influences encouraging the formation of quality circles and development of various teamworking schemes?*

The factors/influences encouraging the formation and introduction of quality circles and team working schemes can be seen to emanate out of the pressures upon organisations to become more competitive, more efficient, more flexible, more concerned with quality; a response to the need to shift towards a system of flexible specialisation and customised quality competitive production. The assumption is that employees do have knowledge and skills to contribute to the organisation of the task and associated processes.

Allied to these pressures are the common "beliefs" that employees both seek and derive satisfaction from being involved and given responsibility and authority. Because employees are more satisfied, they will be more committed to the organisation and its goals and values and committed employees are likely to be more productive, efficient and concerned with the quality of the output.

The influences therefore can be seen to be broadly twofold, one a set of external environmental circumstances and the other derived from a set of beliefs which certainly do not find universal approval, many observers arguing that despite their longevity and popularity amongst management, there is still very little supportive evidence.

Chapter 8

HR Policy and Practice

In this Chapter we focus upon the HR policy areas of recruitment, reward and training and development. We stress the interrelationship between these policy choices, and in investigating comparative approaches to the practice of HRM we find it instructive to connect HR policies to broader structural and cultural features of the societies in question. We draw a broad distinction between "directive" systems, in which the state has considerable visibility in the processes of labour procurement, pay determination and training provision, and "voluntary" systems in which considerable employer discretion and autonomy is allowed in these areas. Nevertheless, across all systems we note two strong trends (see Pieper 1990). The first is a common tendency towards flexibility in work organisation and benefit systems, and the second is individualisation leading to divergent labour needs and HR policies more directed towards individuals.

Discussion Questions

1 How can employers be encouraged to invest in training and development?

A complex question with no easy solution!

In discussing the issues surrounding this, it would be useful to review comparative investment into, and priority attached to training, in various national systems. A reconsideration of Table 8.3 on page 175 and the article by John Authers and Lisa Wood on page 176 would therefore be instructive.

At the centre of the question is the contrast between directive and voluntary approaches. In quite crude terms, it seems that if there is institutional (statutory) or cultural support and encouragement for employers to train (examples of this could be France and Germany) then training assumes a high priority. Where the "voluntary" approach is prevalent and initiatives are largely left to employers, there seems to be a danger that training will be the first item to be cut at a time of recession. The US however may provide a counter to this argument where training is "big business". The focus of this training however seems to be equipping individuals with the competencies to ensure their own, and their corporation's survival.

2 Is high pay consistent or inconsistent with economic performance at corporate and national levels?

Again, this is clearly a matter for debate (and it currently constitutes a political "hot potato"). Discussion in this area may be supplemented by relevant economic and political theory, and useful "fodder" for the debate would be newspaper article "German labour costs almost double UK level" on page 180.

At a corporate level it would seem that the level of pay is but one of a number of factors that may contribute towards, or detract from, success.

The strategy of the organisation in the context of its competitive environment would seem to be significant.

This is illustrated by the successful performance of, in particular, American multinationals which consistently pay above market rates. In contrast, in certain sectors, organisations may gain success by undercutting the competition, perpetuating a low skill labour force.

At an international level, the issues are nowhere better illustrated than in Europe, where the question of pay is at the centre of arguments concerning regulation (associated with harmonisation) and deregulation (associated with the free market)

In essence, those favouring deregulation (notably the UK Government) would argue that competitiveness with other trade blocs can only be achieved through the "realistic" pricing of pay in the market place. On the other hand those in Continental Europe who would favour some regulation of pay (and allied to this a minimum wage) are likely to hold the view that an adequate skill base is vital for future prosperity, and that this can only be achieved through rewarding and investing in staff. Within Europe, these conflicting perspectives have caused tension as the deregulated economies may be viewed as undercutting the higher payers, and attracting investment on that basis. Thus, if we take the case of Germany, its reputation as a high payer has certainly not been at the expense of national economic performance in the past, yet currently rigidities in its wage and salary system are under scrutiny.

3 *Is performance related pay likely to be effective in all cultures? Why/Why not?*

In brief, individual PRP is likely to be most appropriate in less regulated, individualistic cultures, perhaps the US and the UK. It is unlikely to be appropriate in Japan, for example, where it would be viewed as divisive in the context of a "groupist" culture.

More generally, inspection of figure 8.5 on page 179 would suggest that PRP is less likely to be adopted in societies which value egalitarianism and security.

4 *What are the benefits/drawbacks of centralising pay determination from the point of view of (a) employers (b) trade unions?*

From the employers point of view

Advantages

more discretion to local level management; ability to link pay to performance and to local labour market conditions
possibilities to adjust pay to recruit and retain staff
more direct contact with local level employees.

If strategic decisions retained at centre,managerial prerogatives protected through distancing negotiations

Disadvantages

can fragment bargaining effort

may be inflationary due to competitive wage bidding between organisational sub sections/central control may be weakened

line management may not possess necessary negotiating expertise

From the trade union point of view;

Advantages

vests responsibility with those closest to workforce

can relate claims to local market rates and conditions

can benefit from competitive wage bidding/tactical bargaining within organisation

Disadvantages

may distance union influence from corporate decision making

may fragment union organisation

local officials may lack necessary bargaining expertise (see Brian Towers(1993) A Handbook of Industrial Relations Practice. Kogan Page pages 174/175.

SECTION 2

AN OVERVIEW OF NATIONAL SYSTEMS, THE EU AND THE ILO

Notes for Guidance

There are no discussion questions in this Section. Readers are advised to assimilate material from each of the overviews, which are primarily descriptive, and where appropriate, to use case studies as illustrative mechanisms. The purpose of this exercise would be to examine the extent the underlying structural features of the national system are manifested in the case.

The cases may also be used in conjunction with Chapter 8 on HR policy and practice to demonstrate trends identified in practice.

Chapter 20

The Conclusion

Notes for Guidance

In this Chapter, two major issues are explored, and it would be fair to say that the "jury is out" on each of them.

Firstly, the link between HRM and corporate and national performance is explored, and it is concluded that a simple formula cannot be sustained in this respect.

Secondly, whether there is national convergence in the adoption of flexible working practices is considered, and it is concluded that although there are indeed a number of common developments, important institutional, ideological and cultural divisions still exist between nations.